The MISSHAPEN Hamantasch

The Misshapen Hamantasch

A Purim Story

by Rabbi Joseph B. Meszler and Joelle M. Reizes

Illustrated by Kris Graves

PROSPECTIVE PRESS
Winston-Salem

PROSPECTIVE PRESS LLC
Winston-Salem, North Carolina
www.prospectivepress.com
Published in the United States of America by Prospective Press LLC

 TRADEMARK

THE MISSHAPEN HAMANTASCH
Copyright © Joseph B. Meszler and Joelle Reizes, 2024
All rights reserved.
The author's moral rights have been asserted.

Cover and interior art by Kris Graves
© Prospective Press, 2024
The artist's moral right have been asserted.

ISBN 978-1-63516-021-5

ProP-J002

Printed in the United States of America
First Prospective Press hardcover printing, March 2024

The text of this book is typeset in Bubblegum Sans

PUBLISHER'S NOTE:

This story is a work of fiction. The people, names, characters, locations, activities, and events portrayed or implied by this story is the product of the authors imagination or are used fictitiously. Any resemblance to actual people, locations, and events is strictly coincidental. No actual cookies were misshapen in the writing of this book.

Without limiting the rights as reserved in the above copyright, no part of this publication may be reproduced, stored in or introduced into any retrieval system, or transmitted–by any means, in any form, electronic, mechanical, photocopying, recording, or otherwise–without the prior written permission of the publisher. Not only is such reproduction illegal and punishable by law, but it also hurts the authors and illustrator who toiled hard on the creation of this work and the publisher who brought it to the world. In the spirit of fair play, and to honor the labor and creativity of the people who made this book, we ask that you purchase only authorized electronic and paper editions of this work and refrain from participating in or encouraging piracy or electronic piracy of copyright-protected materials. Please give authors a break and don't steal this or any other work.

Dedicated to all people
of every size
and shape

"Roll out your dough!" called the teacher.

The Hebrew School students huddled around a large table. They could not wait to make hamantaschen — special cookies for Purim.

"This is exciting," thought a small ball of dough.

"We will all get some kind of sweet filling, and then each of us will be folded into a triangle. I wonder what kind of filling I will get!"

The dough felt fingers push it into a flat pancake.

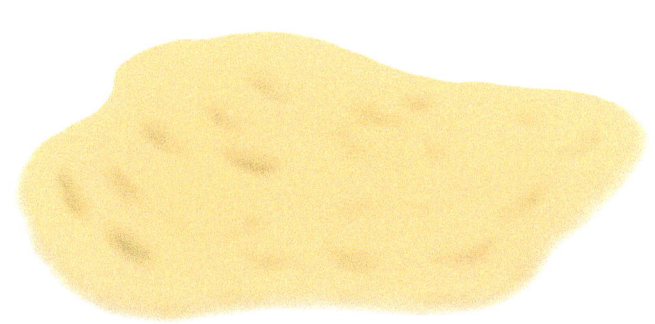

"Wait a second," thought the dough. "I need to be rolled out thinner. I am not spread out enough."

A heaping spoonful of apricot filling plopped onto the dough.

"That's too much!" the dough worried.

"I will never be able to form a triangle and stick together!"

Little hands folded the dough on three sides... sort of.

The hamantasch did not feel good. It felt lumpy in all the wrong places and flat where it should be full.

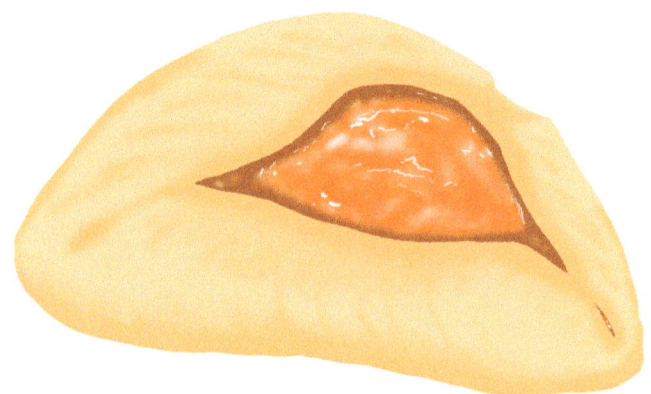

"No one is going to want me like this," it thought.

Different jams filled the rest of the raw cookies — apricot and also raspberry, apple, poppy seed, and prune.

Big hands put the pan into the oven.

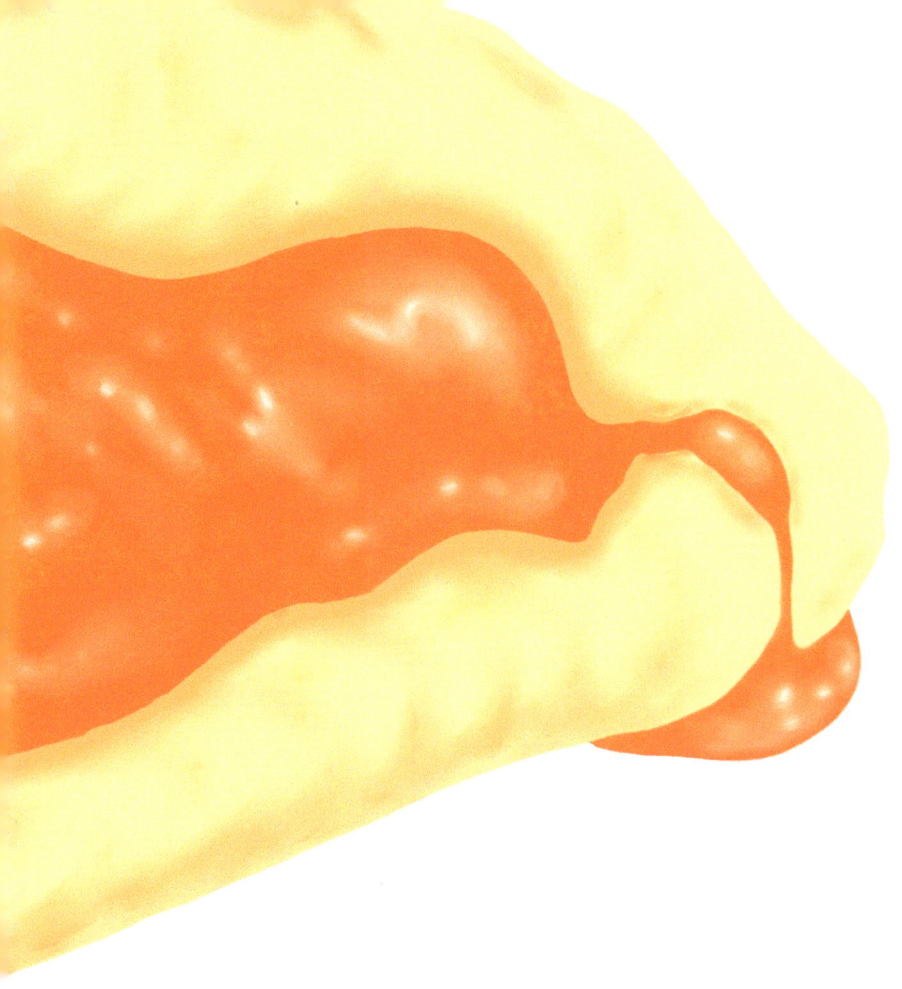

The hamantasch baked, and sure enough, one of its sides burst open.

Its apricot filling leaked.

When it came out into the cool air, it was triangle-like, but it was not perfect.

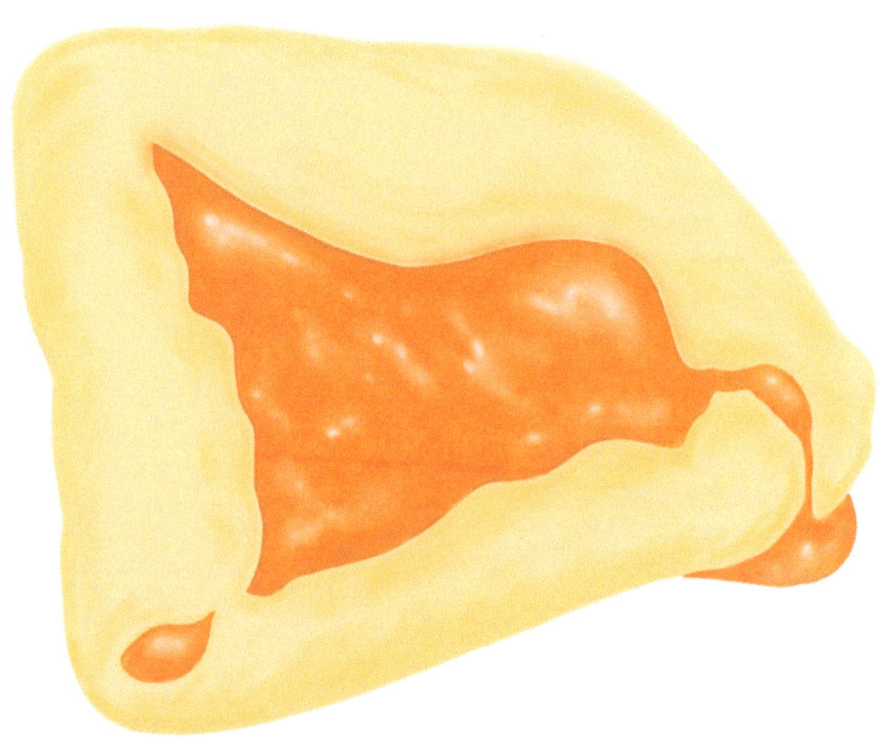

But then the misshapen hamantasch peeked at all the others, and none of them were perfect triangles either.

Each had bumps and leaks.

Still, they all looked... delicious.

Excited voices bounced around them as grownups and children filled the room.

The misshapen hamantasch slid onto a paper plate.

A child's voice yelled, "I made this one for you, Mom!"

A woman looked down at the hamantasch.

"Wow! Thank you. I can see you made it with love."

Now the hamantasch was bursting, not with filling but with joy.

She wrapped up the hamantasch, and the other families took home all the rest of the cookies of every single shape and size.

Hamantaschen (singular – **hamantasch**) are triangular cookies eaten on the holiday of Purim. Purim is a Jewish carnival-like holiday based upon The Book of Esther in the Hebrew Bible. Originally, hamantaschen were pastries filled with poppy seeds ("mohn" in German or Yiddish) and formed into pockets ("taschen"). In Judaism, the cookie became associated with the villain of the story, Haman, through alliteration. Various interpretations of the triangular-shaped cookie claim it symbolizes Haman's pockets, his triangular hat or his ears (Hebrew: *oznei haman*... ew!). Today hamantaschen are made with different kinds of sweet filling. Hebrew School students have been making them for centuries.

About the Author

Rabbi Joseph B. Meszler is the spiritual leader of Temple Sinai in Sharon, MA and a noted Jewish educator and activist. He is the author of several books, educational manuals, and children's stories. He is married with two children. He is Joelle M. Reizes' younger brother, but he is a foot taller.

About the Author

Joelle M. Reizes is a mother of three who writes adult fantasy fiction under the nom de plume, JD Blackrose (www.slipperywords.com). Under that name, she wrote *Seder in Space and Other Tales* and contributed a short story to the *Jewish Book of Horror*, as well as writing other Jewish-themed fiction. She spends much of her time herding words into sentences, trying to get them in the correct order. She is Rabbi Joseph Meszler's big sister, although she is a foot shorter.

About the Artist

Kris Graves has been drawing since they were a tiny sprite. After winning a county-wide art competition in the fourth grade, they set their sights on a life of artistry and cats.

The Misshapen Hamantasch is part of a series published by Prospective Press, including

    The Honey Bee and the Apple Tree: a Rosh Hashanah Story

    Courageous Candles: a Hanukkah Story

    The Sukkah in the Storm: a Sukkot Story

    Two Dinosaurs at Shabbat Dinner

www.ingramcontent.com/pod-product-compliance
Lightning Source LLC
Chambersburg PA
CBHW061126170426
43209CB00014B/1684